UNDER THE MICROSCOPE

OUR BACKYARD

John Woodward

Gareth Stevens Publishing
MILWAUKEE

**For a free color catalog describing Gareth Stevens Publishing's list
of high-quality books and multimedia programs,
call 1-800-542-2595 (USA) or 1-800-461-9120 (Canada).
Gareth Stevens Publishing's Fax: (414) 225-0377.
See our catalog, too, on the World Wide Web: http://gsinc.com**

Library of Congress Cataloging-in-Publication Data

Woodward, John, 1954-
    Our backyard / by John Woodward.
       p. cm. – (Under the microscope)
    Summary: Presents a leaf that breathes through its own pair of lips, soil
teeming with millions of tiny creatures, and many more microscopic marvels.
    Includes index.
    ISBN 0-8368-1600-5 (lib. bdg.)
    1. Natural history–Juvenile literature. [1. Natural history. 2. Microscopy.]
I. Title. II. Series.
QH48.W914   1997
574–dc20   96-34488

First published in North America in 1997 by
Gareth Stevens Publishing
1555 North RiverCenter Drive, Suite 201
Milwaukee, WI 53212 USA

© 1997 Brown Packaging Partworks Ltd., 255-257 Liverpool Road,
London, England, N1 1LX. Text by John Woodward. All photos supplied
by Science Photo Library, except page 9: Frank Lane Picture Agency.
Additional end matter © 1997 by Gareth Stevens, Inc.

Printed in the United States of America

1 2 3 4 5 6 7 8 9 01 00 99 98 97

CONTENTS

BLESSED BACTERIA

Backyard soil is filled with micro-organisms that live on the remains of dead plants and animals. These microorganisms change the dead plants and animals into plant food, which makes soil fertile. The smallest of these soil microorganisms are called bacteria. They are tiny plants made of usually just one cell. Some bacteria cause diseases, but most of them are harmless and essential to life. If they were to be completely destroyed, all other life on Earth would eventually die out.

Soil bacteria forms long threads (*brown*) that grow through the soil and bind soil particles together. Bacteria also produces seeds called spores (*pink*).

TINY PIONEERS

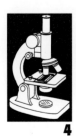

- Bacteria are amazingly tiny. The smallest speck of dust can carry one hundred or more.
- Some forms of bacteria were probably the first living things to appear on our planet. The descendants of these bacteria still live in the hot springs of Yellowstone Park in Wyoming.

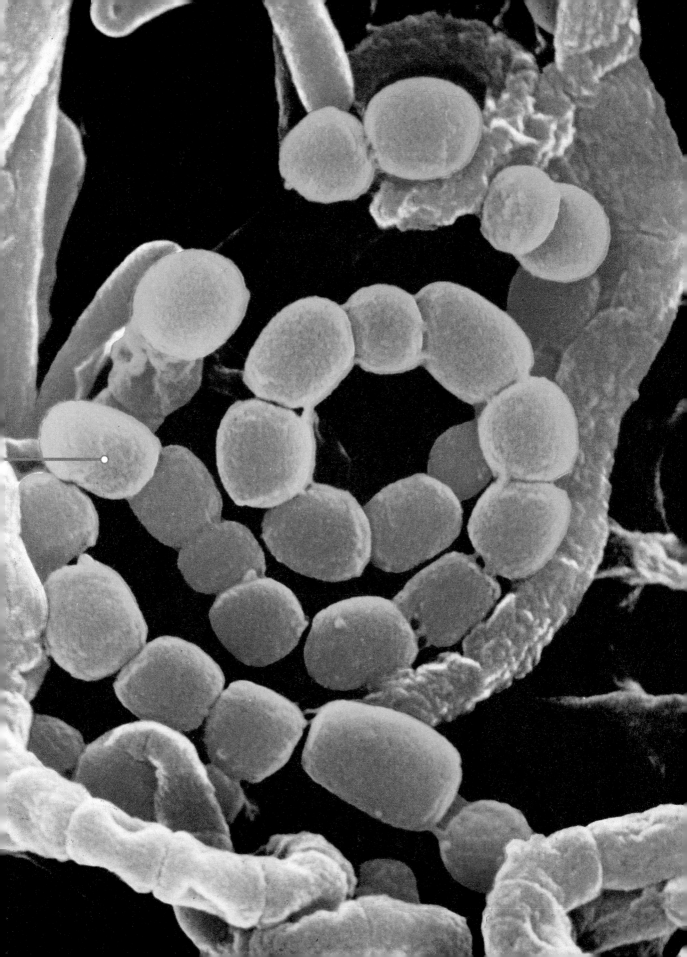

ALGAE ALERT

When pond water turns slimy green in summer, it is likely to be full of microscopic plants called algae. These plants have no roots, no leaves, and no flowers. They are simply chains of cells that soak up plant food from water. When the water becomes warm, algae grow and multiply quickly. Algae turn pond water green, but some types can even turn a pond red. Eventually, the plants die and can all decay at the same time. This uses up all the oxygen in the water, killing the fish and any other animals in the pond.

This is part of an alga called Spyrogyra, which forms slimy threads. The football-shaped objects are spore capsules that contain the "seeds" of new algae.

GIANT ALGAE

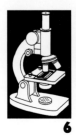

• Many algae are too small to be seen without a microscope, but others are extremely large. These include seaweeds found on beaches and the giant kelp plants that form submerged "forests" off the California coast.

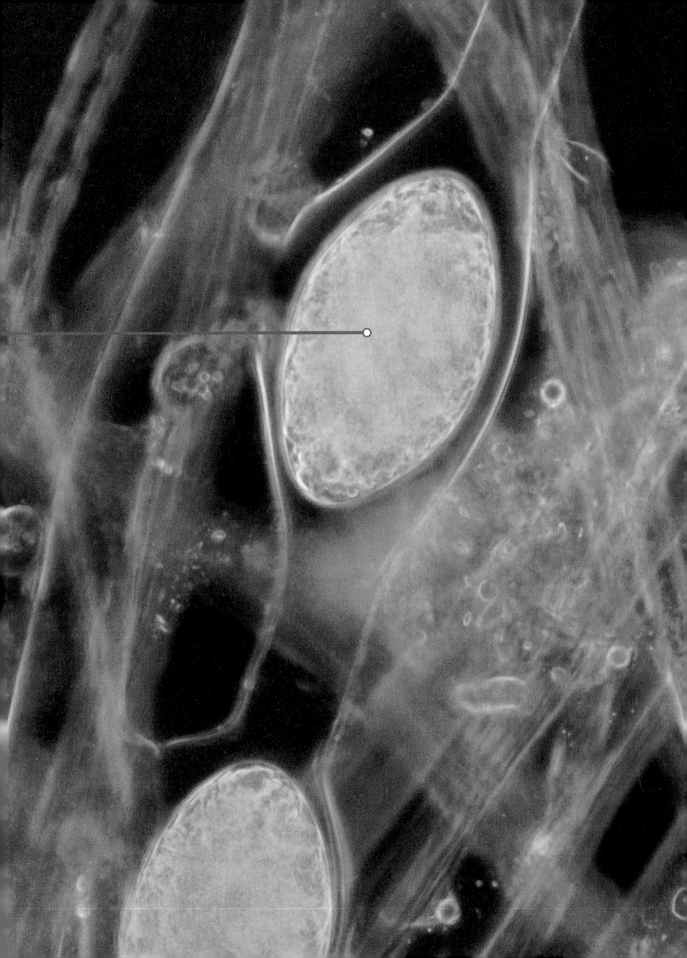

MADE IN THE SHADE

Many ferns look like small trees. But they do not have flowers or seeds like trees have. New fern plants grow from tiny spores that blow in the wind like dust. They are similar to the spores of mushrooms. In order to produce new plants, these spores must land in damp places. That is why ferns are always found in dark, damp spots. Some ferns actually float in water. They can cover entire lakes. In tropical forests, where there is plenty of rain, many types of ferns grow in the tops of trees.

The underside of this fern frond holds special capsules called sori. Sori contain the spores that grow into new fern plants when conditions are wet enough.

FERN FORESTS

- Ferns appeared on Earth long before plants with flowers. About 300 million years ago, there were great fern forests in many parts of the world.
- When these plants died, their remains were preserved and compressed. Over millions of years, the remains turned into coal.

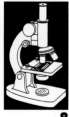

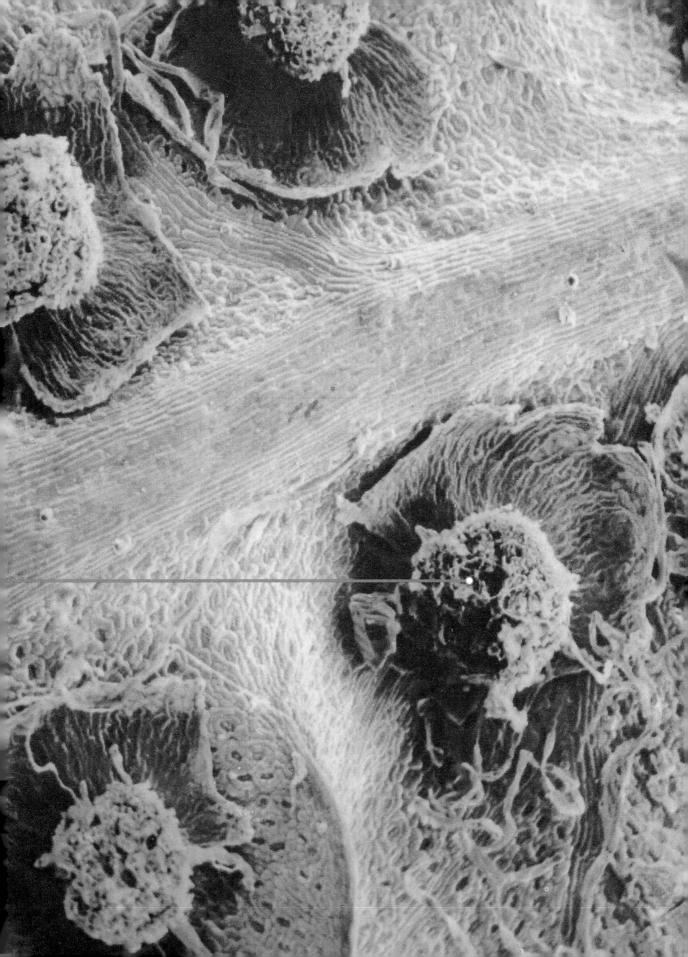

LIFE FORCE

The stem of a flowering plant contains a bundle of tubes. Some of these tubes carry water and food up from the roots. Others carry sugars that are made in the plant's leaves. The entire system for this life force is powered by the heat of the sun. But the heat makes the leaves lose water. This forces the roots to draw more water from the soil. If no water is available, the tubes and all the other tissues of the plant deflate like punctured tires. The plant wilts and collapses — and may die.

This is a slice across the square stem of a nettle plant, specially colored to show its structure. The main tube bundles of the plant are in the large red patches.

WATER PRESSURE

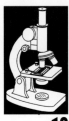

- You can test the importance of water to a plant by putting a cut green-stemmed plant in an empty jar and leaving it in the sun. Before long, the plant will start to wilt. Pour some water in the jar, and the plant will stiffen up again.

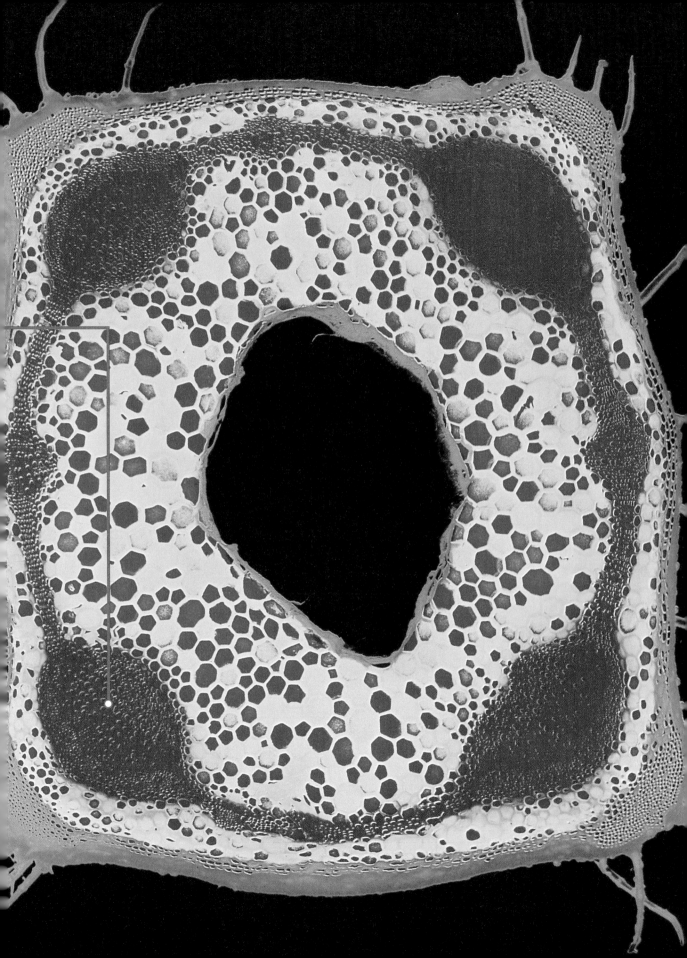

HIGH FIBER

All plants are made of building blocks called cells. Plant cells have tough walls made of a substance called cellulose. This is a type of starch. Cellulose forms strong fibers, like woven fabric. High-fiber foods are made of cellulose fiber. Not only are cellulose fibers strong, they are also flexible. The cellulose in trees is strengthened with another substance called lignin. The mixture forms wood. Because trees have these substances, they are almost rigid, enabling them to grow much taller than other plants.

This slice across the trunk of a sugar maple tree shows woody cells *(yellow)*, food-storing rays *(red)*, and the tubes *(blue)* that carry water up the trunk of the tree.

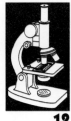

RECORD BREAKERS

- An Australian mountain ash may grow to over an amazing 420 feet (128 meters) tall. The giant sequoias of California grow to 300 feet (91 m) tall.
- A bristlecone pine tree may keep growing for nearly five thousand years.

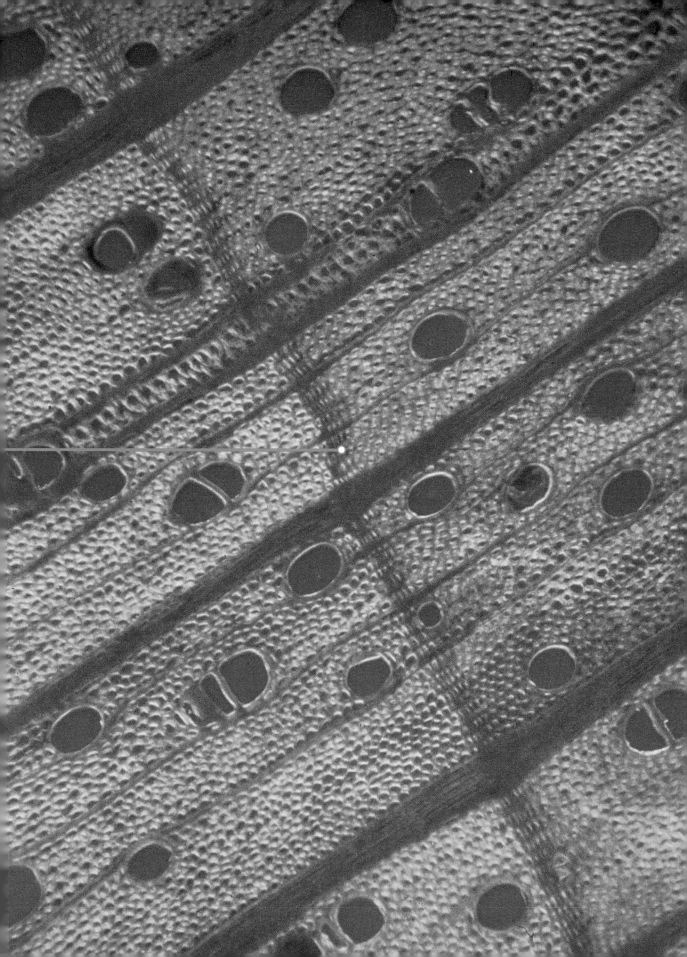

AIR TO SPARE

All plants need oxygen and carbon dioxide from the air. Small water plants usually get enough oxygen and carbon dioxide from the gases dissolved in water. But large water plants have to find other ways of obtaining these substances. For example, water lilies have developed special types of leaves filled with air spaces. This makes the lilies float. Air is absorbed by the floating leaves. The air then passes down to the roots through tubes in the leaf stalks.

This water lily stalk has been sliced off just below one of its floating leaves. In the magnified image, the tubes that carry air down to the plant's roots are visible.

SWAMP SNORKELS

• Some swamp plants have developed creative ways of getting air to their roots. A swamp cypress sends woody spikes up from its roots in the mud. These spikes are actually spongy tubes with small holes that open into the air.

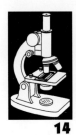

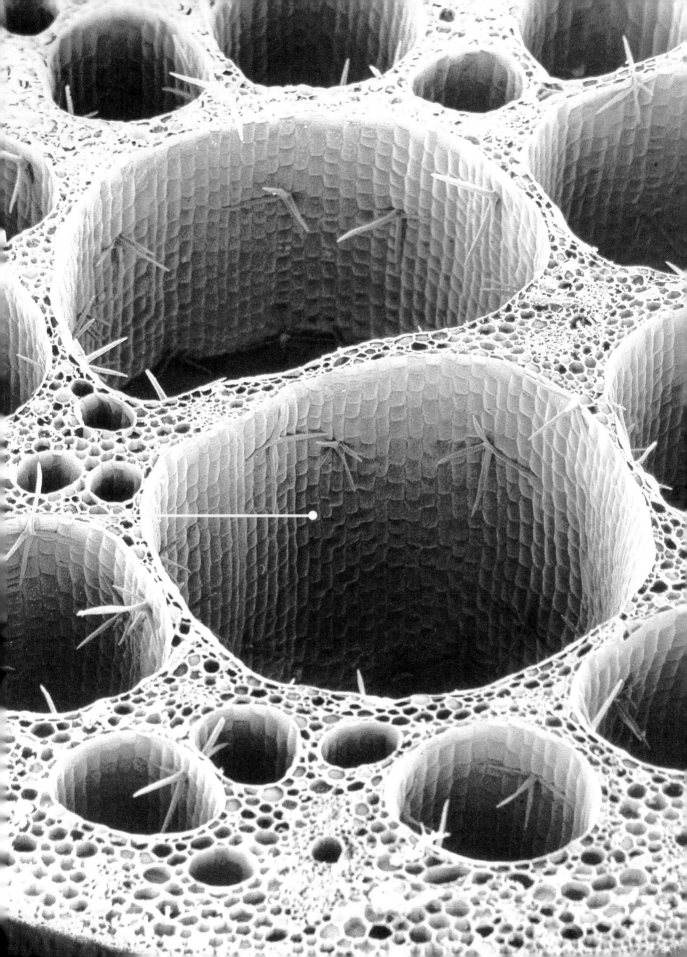

MIGHTY MITES

Most of the tiny, spider-like mites that scurry in the grass are harmless creatures. They feed on debris and other tiny animals. But some mites are bothersome to humans. Young chigger mites, for instance, latch onto people and suck blood from them. This in itself is not harmful. But occasionally, the mite's saliva triggers an allergic reaction in humans, causing an itchy rash that can last for days. In some countries, these creatures also carry an organism called Rickettsia that causes a terrible disease known as scrub-typhus.

Young chigger mites feed on human blood. But adult chigger mites eat other microscopic animals. They prey on them with their powerful jaws.

LYING IN WAIT

- A bloodsucking young mite lurking in the backyard senses when people are near by detecting the carbon dioxide in the air humans breathe out.
- A chigger mite is small enough to slip through the fabric of clothing. It often stops to feed where a belt or waistband prevents it from moving on.

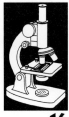

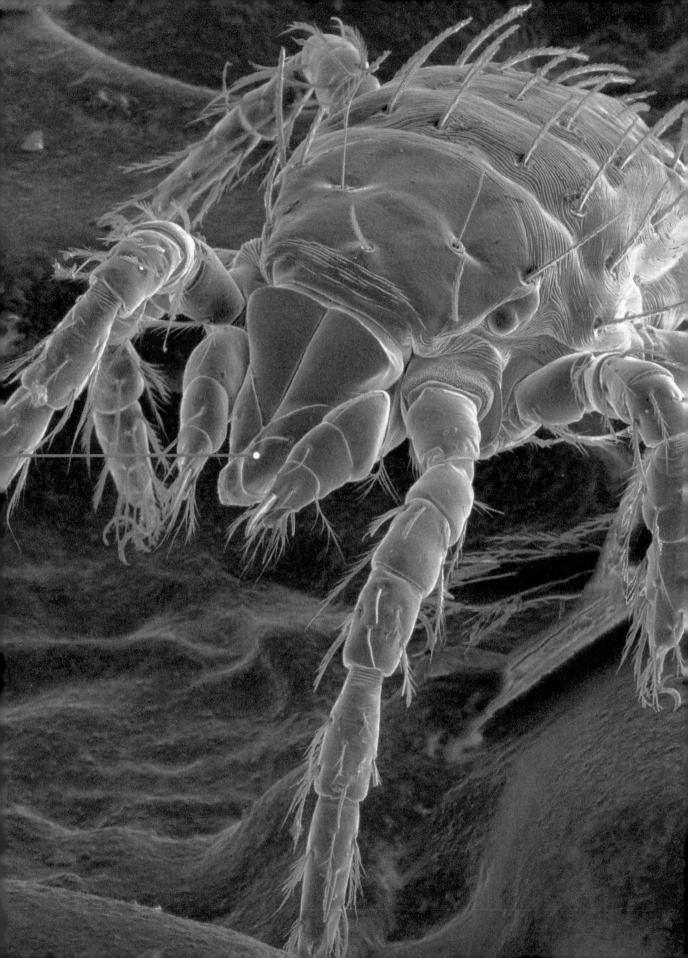

AT THE ROOT

When a seed starts to grow, it first puts down roots. The seed splits open, and a root emerges. Because of gravity, the root turns downward. Then a coat of fine hairs grows at the root's tip. These spread out in the soil and soak up water. If the soil is fertile, the water will contain minerals that feed the plant. As the root tip pushes down, it is protected by a tough cap. This allows it to safely probe between soil particles and rocks and even push its way through cracks in concrete in search of water.

The root tip of this newly sprouted cabbage seed is protected by a strong cap. It needs the protection as it probes the soil in search of water.

SOW AND GROW

• Place some seeds on wet paper toweling, and watch the roots of a new plant develop. Keep the paper toweling moist, and leaves will eventually grow, as well.

FROM DEATH INTO LIFE

Fertile soil is filled with millions of tiny animals. These animals feed on dead plant and animal matter. This helps the processes of decay that turn dead plants and animals into food for living plants. Two of these soil animals are shown here — a mite and a nematode worm. Mites are similar to tiny spiders. They have eight legs and very strong jaws for chewing their food. At least thirty thousand different types of mites exist. Nematodes are tiny worms that have smooth bodies. At least eighty thousand different types of nematodes exist.

A nematode worm investigates a meal mite. The photo has captured a close encounter between just two of the millions of microscopic animals living in the soil.

WORMS CRAWL IN

• Although the microscopic animals living in the soil do a lot of good in the world, they can also be harmful. For instance, nematodes found in tropical countries may live inside the bodies of live animals, including humans, feeding on body tissues.

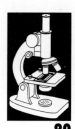

EARTH MOVERS

The soil in our backyards is largely formed due to the action of earthworms. These very helpful animals spend their lives tunneling through soil. They swallow the soil's particles to absorb the food it contains. The tunnels allow air into the ground. This keeps the soil from becoming waterlogged. Earthworms constantly eject bits of waste soil near the surface of the ground. The waste soil is rich in foods that plants need. In areas where there are no earthworms, the soil is infertile. Therefore, many plants cannot survive.

An earthworm has a strong snout for forcing its way through the soil, but it has no eyes. Despite this, it can sense the light, and always burrows away from it.

SINKING STONES

• Earthworms cannot swallow stones, so the soil they eject is smooth and stone-free. Earthworms burrow beneath stones. This causes the stones to gradually sink into the ground.

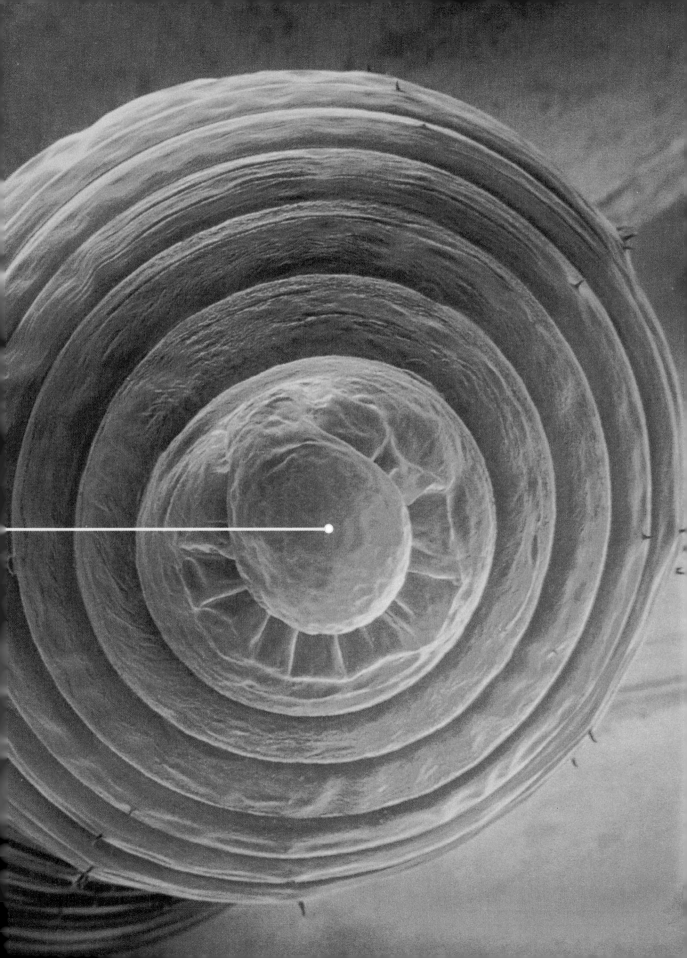

TOOTHFUL WONDERS

The tongue of a garden slug is armed with rows of sharp teeth. As the teeth become dull, they are replaced with new ones — just like the teeth of a shark.

Many of the plants growing in back-yards are eaten by slugs and snails. A slug is simply a snail without a shell. Slugs and snails move in the same way. They glide on a film of mucus produced by a long muscular "foot." Waves of movement ripple down the foot and push the animal along. Slugs and snails feed by scraping plant stems and leaves with their tongues. Their tongues are covered with hard teeth that scrape away plant tissue and carry it into the animal's stomach. New teeth form near the root of the tongue and then push forward to replace old ones.

SNAIL SLIME

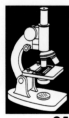

- Put a snail on some glass. When it starts to move, turn the glass upside down and look at the snail from below. Notice the waves of movement rippling down its foot, pushing it along on a silvery trail of mucus. Return the snail safely to the wild.

SOUP FOR SPIDERS

There are many kinds of spiders in backyards. Some build webs, some live in holes, and many just move around. They prey upon tiny animals by attacking them with sharp fangs and injecting poison into them. The prey animals are often then tied up in bundles of silk and gradually eaten. Because a spider can swallow only liquid food, it has to pump special substances into its meal, turning it into a kind of soup. When the spider has finished eating, all that is left of the prey animal is an empty husk.

Most spiders have eight eyes. The eyes of the web-building spider *(pictured)* are tiny, making it almost blind. Its fangs are on the ends of the long jaws under its eyes.

CYBER-SPIDERS

- Spider silk is amazingly strong. A thread of spider silk is stronger than steel wire of the same thickness.
- A spider always builds its web in the same way. It follows a sequence as though a computer program was loaded into its brain at birth.

RUSTING AWAY

Some of the objects in backyards are considered trash. This picture shows a fragment of rusty steel from a damaged car. It has two layers of flaking paint. Steel is a form of iron. Rust is a mixture of iron and oxygen called iron oxide. In nature, iron is found in the form of iron oxide. It is turned into metal in factories. If the metal gets wet, it starts turning back into iron oxide and will eventually decay. It can decay so much that it crumbles to dust. Complete decay takes a long time, however.

This flake of rust from an old car still has the original green paint on it. The blue paint was added later. The rust is much thicker than the metal it replaces.

RUSTPROOFING

• In wet countries like Ireland, steel rusts quickly. In very dry air, however, steel hardly rusts at all. In Arabia, for example, machines that were abandoned in the desert eighty years ago are still in quite good condition.

GLOSSARY

algae: simple plant-like organisms with no roots. Each one is an alga.

bacteria: single-celled organisms that move like animals but make their food like plants.

carbon dioxide: a mixture of carbon and oxygen that forms a gas.

cell: the basic building-block of every plant and animal.

cellulose: the tough material that forms the walls of plant cells.

decay: the process by which materials are broken down.

fangs: hollow "teeth" used by certain animals to inject poison.

fertile: rich in the substances needed for creating life.

lignin: the substance that strengthens cellulose to make wood.

microorganism: a living being so tiny that it can be seen only with a microscope.

mineral: a natural material in the soil that plants need to survive.

mucus: slime exuded by animals such as slugs and snails.

organism: a living being of any kind.

sori: capsules on a fern that contain spores that grow into new ferns.

spore: a tiny "seed" of a fern or mushroom.

tissue: any material made of plant or animal cells, such as wood or skin.

FURTHER STUDY

BOOKS

Bloodthirsty Plants (series). Victor Gentle (Gareth Stevens)

Close Up: Microscopic Photographs of Everyday Stuff. Frank B. Edwards (Firefly Books)

Compost Critters. Bianca Lavies (Dutton)

Earthworms. Barrie Watts (Franklin Watts)

Eco-Journey (series). Behm/Bonar (Gareth Stevens)

The New Creepy Crawly Collection (series). (Gareth Stevens)

Rocks and Soil. Terry Jennings (Childrens)

Under the Ground. Henry Pluckrose (Childrens)

VIDEOS

Animal Families series: The Crayfish. The Frog. The Snail. The Spider. The Turtle. (Barr Films)

Backyard Science (series). (Phoenix/BFA)

Bacteria. (Encyclopædia Britannica)

Kinds of Plants. Microscopic Pond Life. Animals and Such (series). (Agency for Instructional Technology)

Making the Unseen Visible. Images and Things (series). (Agency for Instructional Technology)

The Microscopic Pond. (Educational Images)

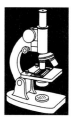

INDEX

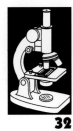